SCHOLASTIC

GRAPHIC ORGANIZER BOOKLETS
for *Reading Response*

Guided Response Packets for Any Fiction or Nonfiction Book That Boost Students' Comprehension—and Help You Manage Independent Reading

by Rhonda Graff Silver

NEW YORK • TORONTO • LONDON • AUCKLAND • SYDNEY
MEXICO CITY • NEW DELHI • HONG KONG • BUENOS AIRES

Teaching *Resources*

To Craig, Daniel, Jackie, Holly, Ruth and Ro

Cover design by Jason Robinson
Interior design by Melinda Belter
Interior illustrations by Teresa Anderko

ISBN-13 978-0-439-65612-2
ISBN-10 0-439-65612-5

Table of Contents

INTRODUCTION 4

NONFICTION

    Biography 8

    Nonfiction 15

    Animal Acts 22

FICTION

    Fairy Tales 29

    Fables/Tales 36

    Fiction 43

    Fiction 50

    Mystery 57

Introduction

Using visual aids goes well beyond having students fill in worksheets. The graphic organizers in this book will help students learn necessary skills, actively participate in learning, and take part in discussions, all of which result in higher levels of thinking.

The Benefits of Using This Book

There are many benefits for teachers and students who use visual representations such as graphic organizers, webs, and maps.

➤ Organizers help students focus on key points instead of overwhelming them with pages of information.

➤ Organizers encourage students to make connections, identify relationships, and see information in new ways.

➤ When organizers are used, students think and write about what they read. They have the opportunity to share what they've read as they discuss their responses on the organizers.

How to Use This Book

This book is arranged into eight six-page student booklets. Each booklet focuses on either a genre or a theme related to nonfiction or fiction. The booklets can be reproduced back-to-back and then stapled together to form a spine.

A teacher page accompanies each booklet. This page includes:

➤ reduced pages with sample answers based on an exemplary text.

➤ instructional points, discussion starters, and/or teacher tips

Each student booklet contains a cover page, related activity pages, and a personal response page.

➤ The cover page includes space for students to fill in information about the book or resource being used and a space for them to record their prior knowledge or related personal experience.

➤ The middle pages consist of related organizers, charts, and webs.

➤ The last page of each booklet is a personal response page, allowing students to integrate the knowledge they attained from the study with personal ideas, thoughts, questions, and discussion prompts. (NOTE: It's important for students to provide personal responses, but be sure they are using the new information related to their study and not overusing unrelated, personal judgments.)

Background Information

Although detailed directions appear on each page of a booklet, students will still need direct and explicit instruction in order to learn how to complete these graphic organizer activities successfully and meaningfully. Sharing a completed organizer and modeling the process of completion will benefit students and move them toward independence. It is important to model not only "how to" but also to model the thinking process that occurs as an activity is completed. As with all skills, practice and feedback are crucial to achieving automaticity.

It is not necessary to require an in-depth response for every book that students read. However, when students choose a book to use with a booklet, they should understand that the focus should not be on completing every question on every page, but rather on the importance of discussing, questioning, and learning from peers. The goal is to achieve a higher level of thinking and understanding. Always encourage students to elaborate and explain their responses. Use the organizers to help them plan, organize, and share information about what they've read and learned. Note students' different strengths and how they are able to share what they really know. The feedback and interaction will help promote true learning and growth.

Students should discuss how the organizers worked for them, noting possible changes to the visuals they present. Their creativity may offer new insight and alternative ways of meeting the goals. Students should be encouraged to create their own graphic organizers to assist in their learning. If these activities are to foster higher-level thinking, then students must be guided in that direction.

The literacy organizers in this book support the following standards outlined by the New York State Education Department Virtual Learning System and the Mid-continental Regional Educational Laboratory

(McREL). (Other state and regional standards can certainly be supported as well, however, due to the variety of standards across different geographical areas, it's not easy to compile a comprehensive list of standards.) As they work with the organizers, students will do the following:

- ❧ read, write, listen, and speak for information and understanding

- ❧ read, write, listen, and speak for literacy expression

- ❧ read, write, listen, and speak for critical analysis and evaluation

- ❧ read, write, listen, and speak for social interaction

- ❧ gather and use information for research purposes

- ❧ use the general skills and strategies of the reading process

- ❧ use reading skills and strategies to understand and interpret a variety of literary texts

- ❧ use reading skills and strategies to understand and interpret a variety of informational texts

- ❧ use listening and speaking strategies for different purposes

When students read with a goal in mind, they will be more likely to focus on what they are reading. The purpose of using these graphic organizer booklets is to have students internalize these skills so that they will be better able to organize their own thoughts, ideas, and questions. With experience, students can begin to create their own graphic organizers.

Hopefully, the optimal outcome is having students become strong, critical readers who truly enjoy reading and learning. With this framework, students can better understand what they read throughout their school years and into adulthood.

Helpful Hints for the Biography Booklet:

- Model each activity as many times as necessary to ensure that students fully understand objectives and directions before working independently or in groups.

- Remind students to preview the booklet so they are aware of pre-reading, during-reading, and post-reading activities. For example, page 2 requires both pre-reading and post-reading responses.

- On page 3, you may need to clarify the concept of a dialogue bubble versus a thought bubble.

- Encourage students to reflect and discuss using the *For Thought and Discussion* questions on page 6.

Exemplary text: *NBA Superstar Shaquille O'Neal* by Lyle Spencer (Scholastic, 2002)

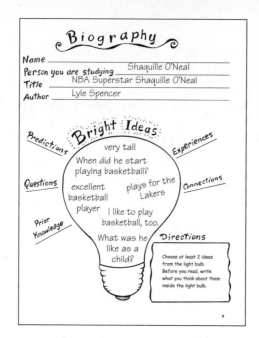

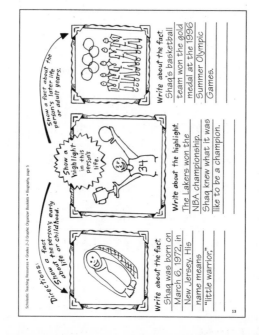

Biography

Name _____

Person you are studying _____

Title _____

Author _____

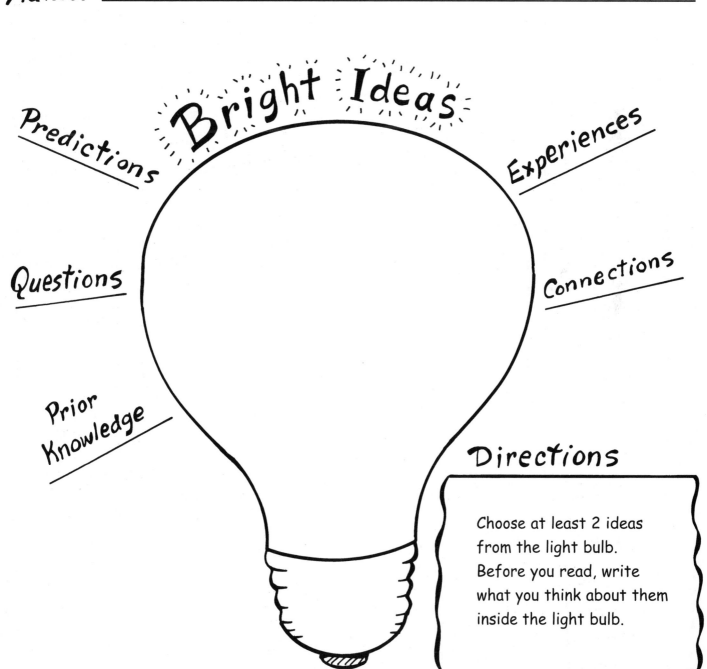

Bright Ideas

Predictions

Experiences

Questions

Connections

Prior Knowledge

Directions

Choose at least 2 ideas from the light bulb. Before you read, write what you think about them inside the light bulb.

Directions

Before reading, write 1 question about this person in each question box.
As you read, gather important facts to answer each question.

Question 1

Answer 1

When you finish reading, write your answer to Question 1.

Question 2

Answer 2

When you finish reading, write your answer to Question 2.

Scholastic Teaching Resources • Grades 2–3 Graphic Organizer Booklets • Biography, page 2

Person _____

Dialogue Bubble

Thought Bubble

Directions

In the dialogue bubble, write what this person would say.

In the thought bubble, write what this person would think.

Color the figures to look like the person you are studying.

Lights! BIOGRAPHY! Action!

Directions

Describe some important things this person has done.

Share your response.

Draw a picture.	Write.
	_____
	_____
	_____
	_____
	_____
	_____
	_____
	_____
	_____
	_____

Scholastic Teaching Resources • Grades 2–3 Graphic Organizer Booklets • Biography, page 4

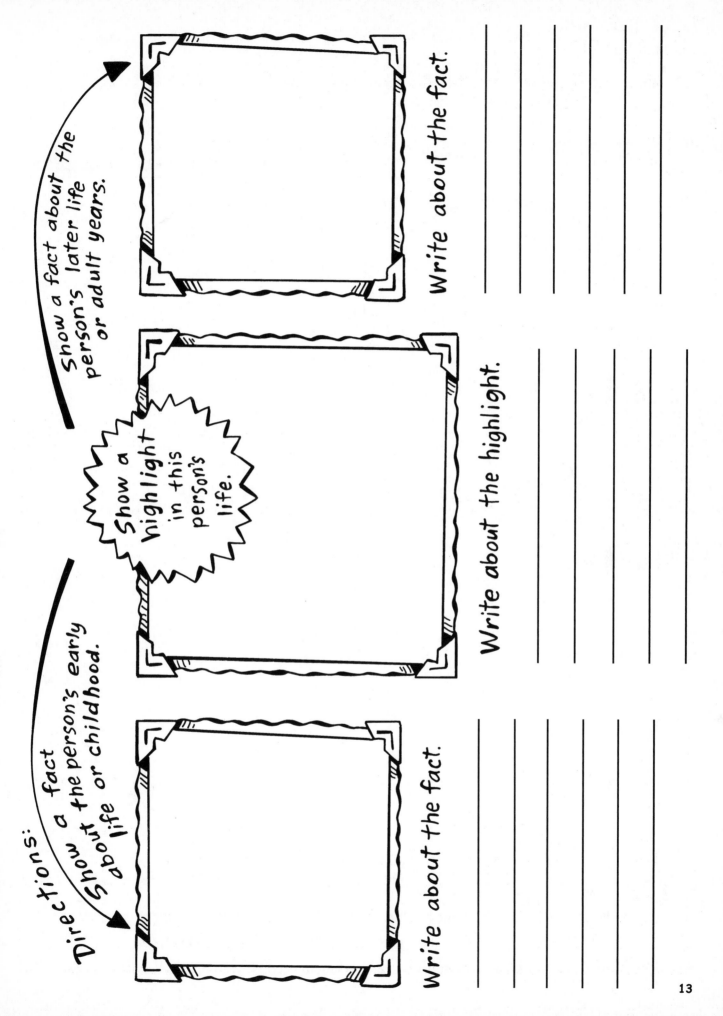

Directions:

Show a fact about the person's early life or childhood.

Show a highlight in this person's life.

Show a fact about the person's later life or adult years.

Write about the fact.

Write about the highlight.

Write about the fact.

Directions

Compare and contrast yourself to the person you studied.
How are you alike? How are you different?

★ **You** _____

★ **Person**
Studied _____

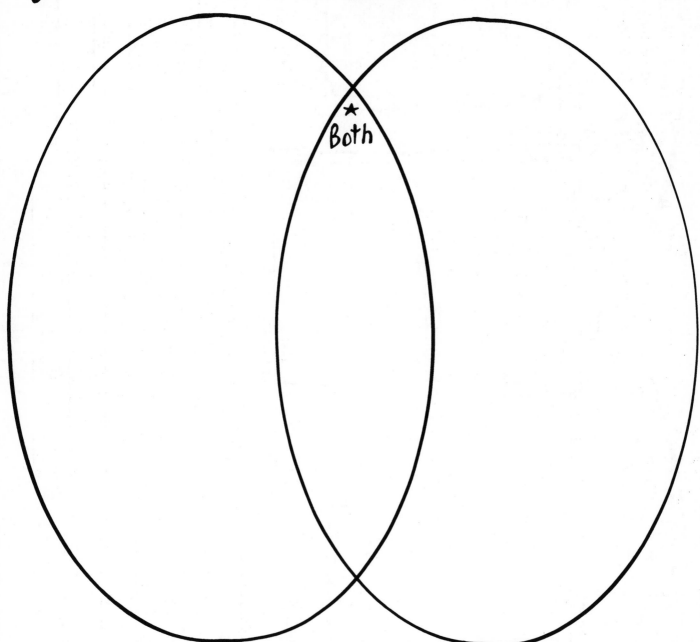

★
Both

For Thought and Discussion

- If you could meet this person, what would you ask him or her?
- What did you find most interesting about this person?
- What other biographies of famous people would you like to read?

Scholastic Teaching Resources • Grades 2–3 Graphic Organizer Booklets • Biography, page 6

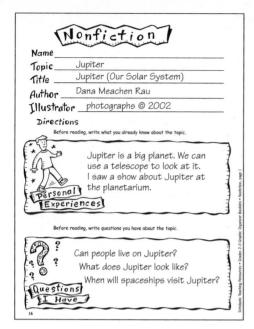

Nonfiction

Name _____

Topic _____ Jupiter

Title _____ Jupiter (Our Solar System)

Author _____ Dana Meachen Rau

Illustrator _____ photographs © 2002

Directions

Before reading, write what you already know about the topic.

Jupiter is a big planet. We can use a telescope to look at it. I saw a show about Jupiter at the planetarium.

Personal Experiences

Before reading, write questions you have about the topic.

Can people live on Jupiter?
What does Jupiter look like?
When will spaceships visit Jupiter?

Questions I Have

16

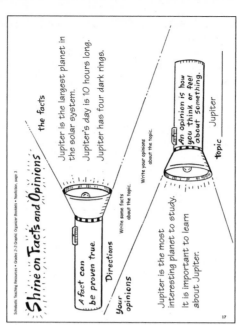

Shine on Facts and Opinions

the facts

Jupiter is the largest planet in the solar system.
Jupiter's day is 10 hours long.
Jupiter has four dark rings.

Directions

A fact can be proven true.

Your opinions

Write some facts about the topic.

An opinion is how you think or feel about something.

Write your opinions about the topic.

Jupiter is the most interesting planet to study. It is important to learn about Jupiter.

topic _____ Jupiter

17

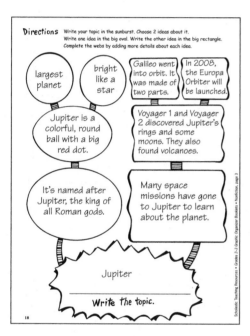

Directions Write your topic in the sunburst. Choose 2 ideas about it. Write one idea in the big oval. Write the other idea in the big rectangle. Complete the webs by adding more details about each idea.

largest planet

bright like a star

Galileo went into orbit. It was made of two parts.

In 2008, the Europa Orbiter will be launched.

Jupiter is a colorful, round ball with a big red dot.

Voyager 1 and Voyager 2 discovered Jupiter's rings and some moons. They also found volcanoes.

It's named after Jupiter, the king of all Roman gods.

Many space missions have gone to Jupiter to learn about the planet.

Jupiter

Write the topic.

18

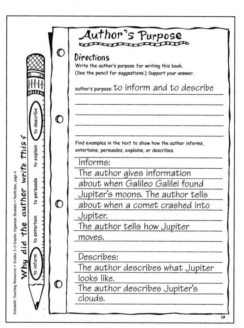

Author's Purpose

Directions

Write the author's purpose for writing this book. (See the pencil for suggestions.) Support your answer.

author's purpose: to inform and to describe

_____
_____
_____

Why did the author write this?
to describe / to explain / to entertain / to persuade / to inform

Find examples in the text to show how the author informs, entertains, persuades, explains, or describes.

Informs:
The author gives information about when Galileo Galilei found Jupiter's moons. The author tells about when a comet crashed into Jupiter.
The author tells how Jupiter moves.

Describes:
The author describes what Jupiter looks like.
The author describes Jupiter's clouds.

19

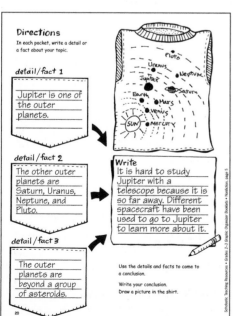

Directions

In each pocket, write a detail or a fact about your topic.

detail/fact 1
Jupiter is one of the outer planets.

detail/fact 2
The other outer planets are Saturn, Uranus, Neptune, and Pluto.

detail/fact 3
The outer planets are beyond a group of asteroids.

Pluto, Uranus, Jupiter, Neptune, Earth, Saturn, Mars, Venus, Mercury, SUN

Write
It is hard to study Jupiter with a telescope because it is so far away. Different spacecraft have been used to go to Jupiter to learn more about it.

Use the details and facts to come to a conclusion.

Write your conclusion.

Draw a picture in the shirt.

20

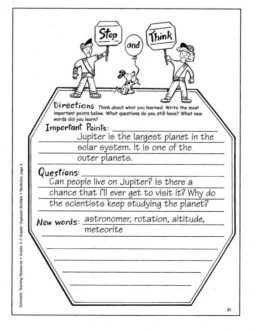

Stop and Think

Directions Think about what you learned. Write the most important points below. What questions do you still have? What new words did you learn?

Important Points: _____
Jupiter is the largest planet in the solar system. It is one of the outer planets.

Questions: _____
Can people live on Jupiter? Is there a chance that I'll ever get to visit it? Why do the scientists keep studying the planet?

New words: astronomer, rotation, altitude, meteorite

_____
_____

21

Helpful Hints for the Nonfiction Booklet:

- Model each activity so students fully understand objectives and directions before they work independently or in groups.

- Preview the booklet with students to be sure they are aware of pre-reading, during reading, and post-reading activities.

- Before students begin work on page 4, point out that an author may have more than one purpose.

- As students reflect and share, stretch their thinking to encourage "why" questions, application of new principles, description, judgments, and problem solving.

Exemplary text: *Jupiter (Our Solar System)* by Dana Meachen Rau (Compass Point Books, 2002)

Nonfiction

Name _____

Topic _____

Title _____

Author _____

Illustrator _____

Directions

Before reading, write what you already know about the topic.

Before reading, write questions you have about the topic.

Scholastic Teaching Resources • Grades 2–3 Graphic Organizer Booklets • Nonfiction, page 1

Shine on Facts and Opinions

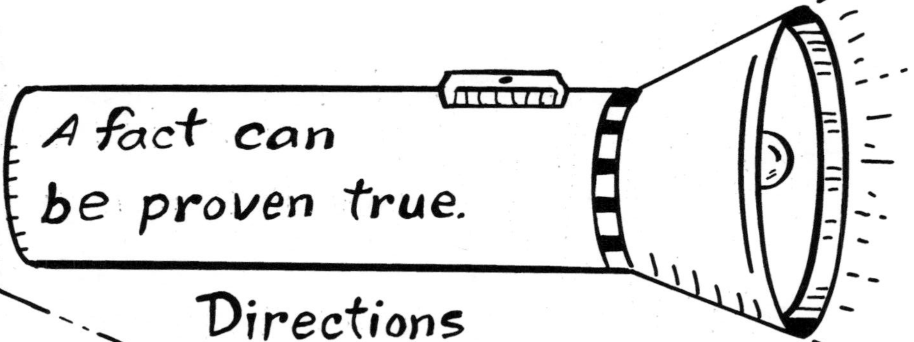

the facts

A fact can be proven true.

Directions

Write some facts about the topic.

Your opinions

Write your opinions about the topic.

An opinion is how you think or feel about something.

topic

Directions Write your topic in the sunburst. Choose 2 ideas about it.
Write one idea in the big oval. Write the other idea in the big rectangle.
Complete the webs by adding more details about each idea.

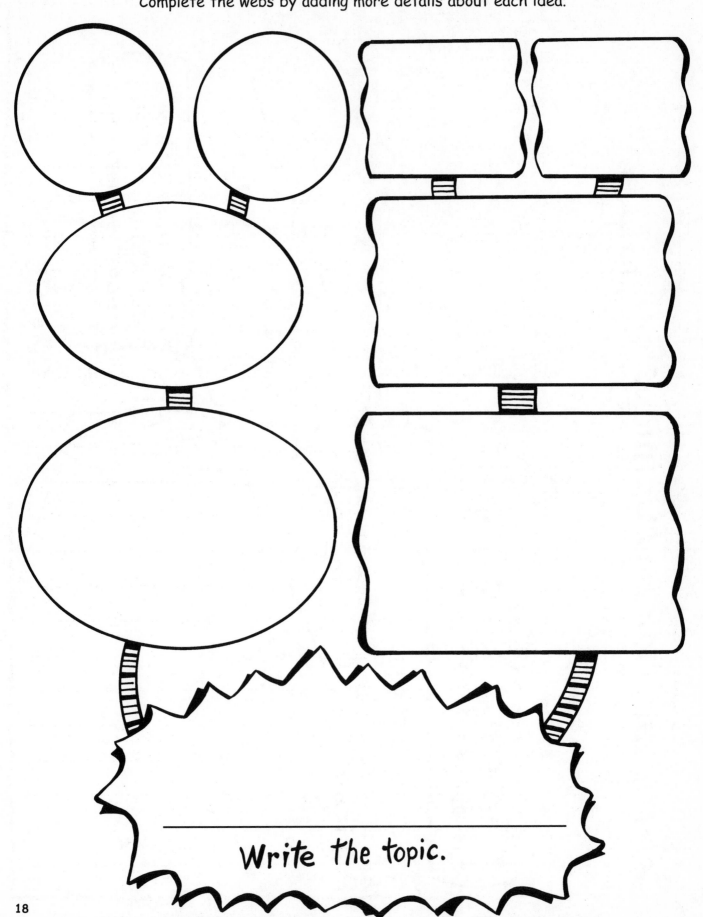

Write the topic.

Scholastic Teaching Resources • Grades 2–3 Graphic Organizer Booklets • Nonfiction, page 3

Author's Purpose

Directions

Write the author's purpose for writing this book.
(See the pencil for suggestions.) Support your answer.

author's purpose:

_____

_____

_____

_____

_____

Find examples in the text to show how the author informs,
entertains, persuades, explains, or describes.

_____

_____

_____

_____

_____

_____

_____

_____

_____

_____

_____

Why did the author write this?

to describe   to explain   to persuade   to entertain   to inform

Directions

In each pocket, write a detail or a fact about your topic.

detail/fact 1

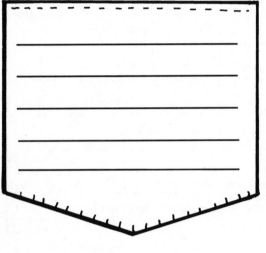

detail/fact 2

detail/fact 3

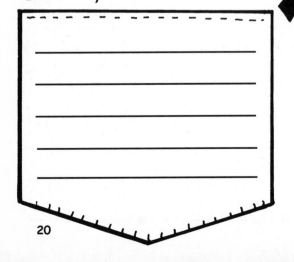

Write

Use the details and facts to come to a conclusion.

Write your conclusion.
Draw a picture in the shirt.

Scholastic Teaching Resources • Grades 2–3 Graphic Organizer Booklets • Nonfiction, page 5

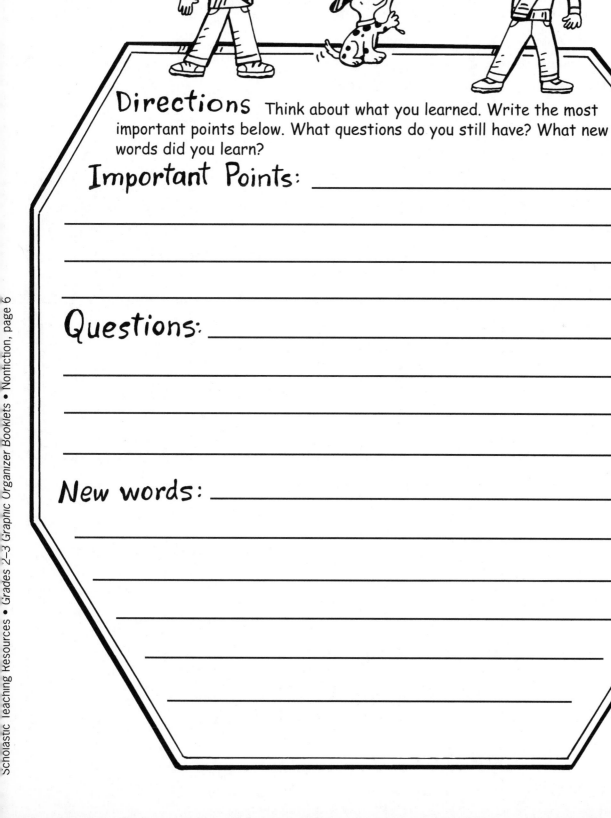

Directions Think about what you learned. Write the most important points below. What questions do you still have? What new words did you learn?

Important Points: _____

_____

_____

_____

Questions: _____

_____

_____

_____

New words: _____

_____

_____

_____

Scholastic Teaching Resources • Grades 2–3 Graphic Organizer Booklets • Nonfiction, page 6

Helpful Hints for the Animal Acts Booklet:

- Model each activity to ensure that students fully understand objectives and directions before they work independently or in groups.

- Remind students to preview the booklet to be sure they identify pre-reading, during-reading, and post-reading activities.

- This booklet can be used to help students "take notes." Students should preview the booklet to see what information can be recorded. As they read, they can use sticky notes to highlight areas of interest in the text and later fill in the booklet with this information.

- This booklet can also aid students in organizing and planning a written activity or report.

Exemplary text: *Polar Bears* by Gail Gibbons (Holiday House, 2001)

Animal Acts

Name _____
Animal   polar bears
Resources (books, magazines, websites) _____
Polar Bears by Gail Gibbons © 2001
www.enchantedlearning.com
_____

Directions
Write what you know about the animal you are studying.

big   white bears

live in cold areas   swim in cold water

see at the zoo

babies are called cubs

23

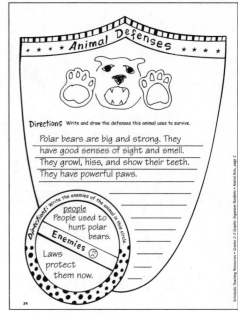

Animal Defenses

Directions Write and draw the defenses this animal uses to survive.

Polar bears are big and strong. They have good senses of sight and smell. They growl, hiss, and show their teeth. They have powerful paws.

Directions: Write the enemies of the animal in this circle.

Enemies

people
People used to hunt polar bears.
Laws protect them now.

24

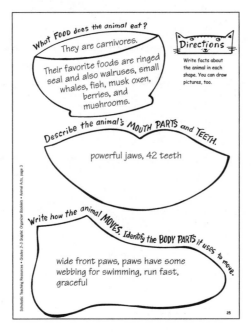

What FOOD does the animal eat?
They are carnivores.
Their favorite foods are ringed seal and also walruses, small whales, fish, musk oxen, berries, and mushrooms.

Directions
Write facts about the animal in each shape. You can draw pictures, too.

Describe the animal's MOUTH PARTS and TEETH.
powerful jaws, 42 teeth

Write how the animal MOVES. Identify the BODY PARTS it uses to move.
wide front paws, paws have some webbing for swimming, run fast, graceful

25

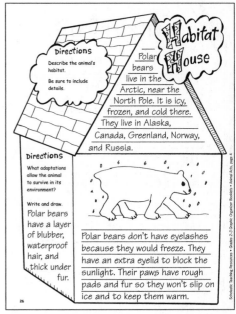

Directions
Describe the animal's habitat.
Be sure to include details.

Habitat House

Polar bears live in the Arctic, near the North Pole. It is icy, frozen, and cold there. They live in Alaska, Canada, Greenland, Norway, and Russia.

Directions
What adaptations allow the animal to survive in its environment?
Write and draw.
Polar bears have a layer of blubber, waterproof hair, and thick under fur.

Polar bears don't have eyelashes because they would freeze. They have an extra eyelid to block the sunlight. Their paws have rough pads and fur so they won't slip on ice and to keep them warm.

26

Directions
Draw the animal in the large box. Label the important parts of the animal. In the small boxes, write details or key words that support the details in your drawing.

Classification/Group
mammal · bird · fish · amphibian · reptile
mammals

Size
when standing on hind legs, 10 feet weighs 750 pounds

Body Covering
fur: colorless hairs that look white, under fur

Babies/Young Animals
called cubs, 1-4 cubs born in winter, weigh about 1 pound

Other
Cubs drink mother's milk.

polar bear
animal name

27

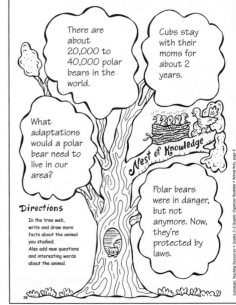

There are about 20,000 to 40,000 polar bears in the world.

Cubs stay with their moms for about 2 years.

What adaptations would a polar bear need to live in our area?

Nest of Knowledge

Polar bears were in danger, but not anymore. Now, they're protected by laws.

Directions
In the tree web, write and draw more facts about the animal you studied. Also add new questions and interesting words about the animal.

28

Animal Acts

Name _____

Animal _____

Resources (books, magazines, websites) _____

_____

_____

_____

Directions

Write what you know about the animal you are studying.

Animal Defenses

Directions Write and draw the defenses this animal uses to survive.

_____

_____

_____

_____

_____

_____

_____

_____

_____

_____

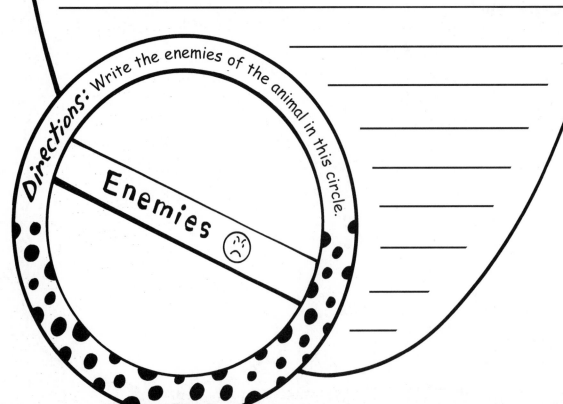

Directions: Write the enemies of the animal in this circle.

Enemies

Scholastic Teaching Resources • Grades 2–3 Graphic Organizer Booklets • Animal Acts, page 2

What FOOD does the animal eat?

Write facts about
the animal in each
shape. You can draw
pictures, too.

Describe the animal's MOUTH PARTS and TEETH.

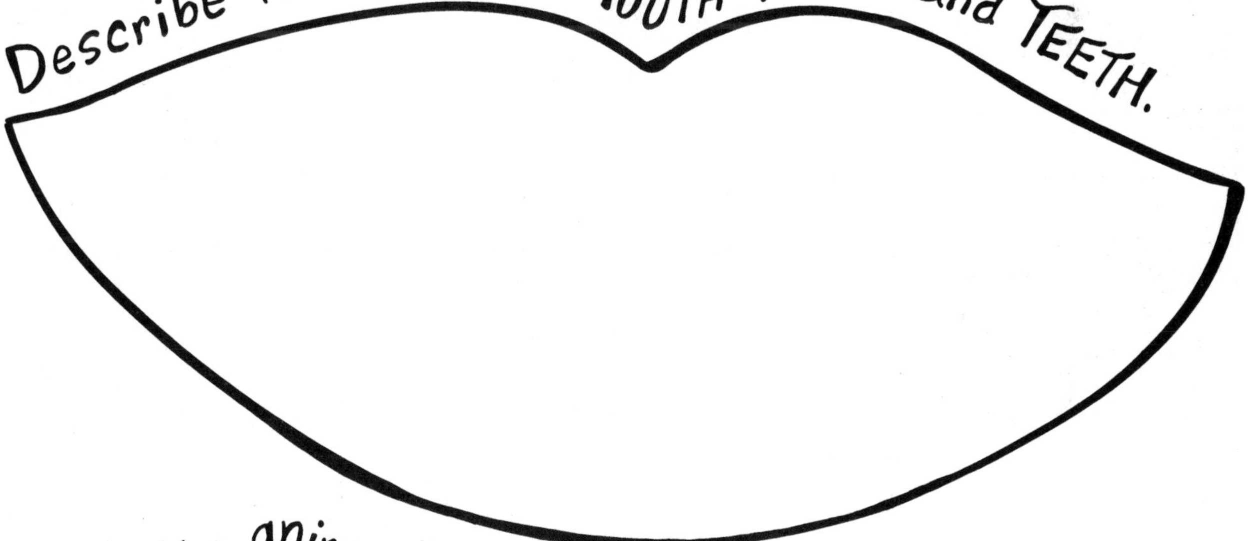

Write how the animal MOVES. Identify the BODY PARTS it uses to move.

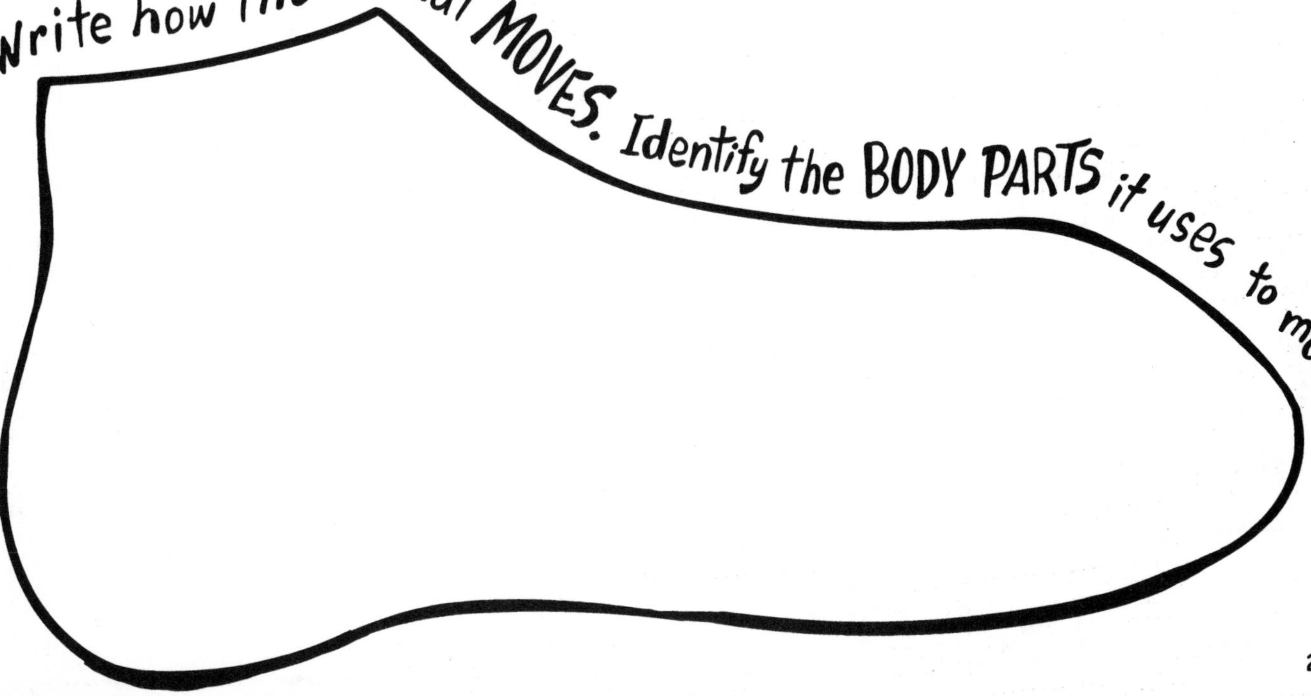

Directions

Describe the animal's habitat.

Be sure to include details.

Habitat House

Directions

What adaptations allow the animal to survive in its environment?

Write and draw.

Scholastic Teaching Resources • Grades 2–3 Graphic Organizer Booklets • Animal Arts page 4

Directions

Draw the animal in the large box. Label the important parts of the animal. In the small boxes, write details or key words that support the details in your drawing.

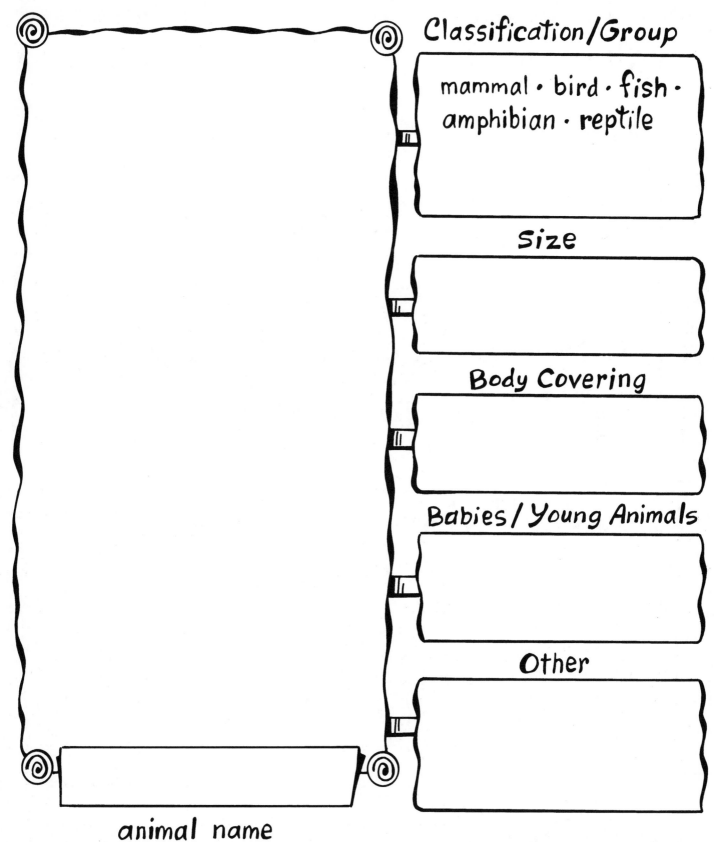

Classification/Group

mammal · bird · fish · amphibian · reptile

Size

Body Covering

Babies / Young Animals

Other

animal name

Scholastic Teaching Resources • Grades 2–3 Graphic Organizer Booklets • Animal Acts, page 5

Nest of Knowledge

Directions

In the tree web,
write and draw more
facts about the animal
you studied.
Also add new questions
and interesting words
about the animal.

Scholastic Teaching Resources • Grades 2–3 Graphic Organizer Booklets • Animal Arts, page 6

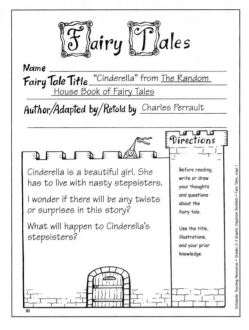

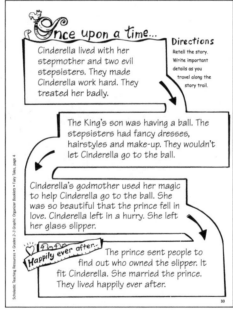

Helpful Hints for the Fairy Tales Booklet:

- Model each activity until students fully understand objectives and directions before they begin working independently or in groups.

- Remind students to preview the booklet to be sure they are aware of pre-reading, during-reading, and post-reading activities.

- On page 2, have students clarify *why* they classified each character as good or evil. Ask them to use the text to support their positions.

- On page 5, students compare fairy tales. This gives them exposure to multiple fairy tales and helps them think about the story plot.

- Encourage reflection and discussion.

Exemplary text: *The Random House Book of Fairy Tales* adapted by Amy Ehrlich (Random House, 1985)

Fairy Tales

Name _____

Fairy Tale Title _____

_____

Author/Adapted by/Retold by _____

_____

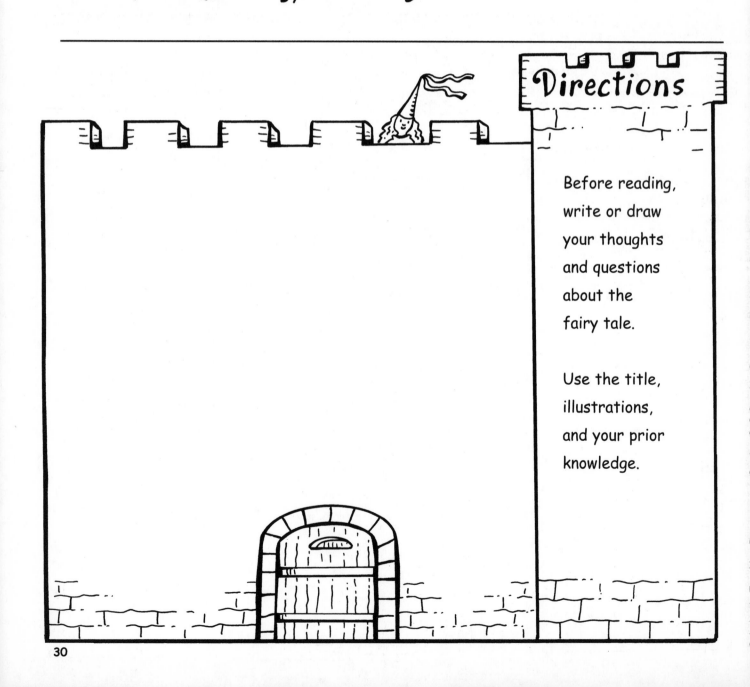

Directions

Before reading, write or draw your thoughts and questions about the fairy tale.

Use the title, illustrations, and your prior knowledge.

Fairy tales have good
and evil characters.

Good

Evil

Directions

Write about and draw the good characters
in this tale.

Directions

Write about and draw the evil characters
in this tale.

Magic in Fairy Tales

Directions

Is there any magic in this tale? Write about it.

Think about—

Who	What
Where	When
Why	How

Illustrate.

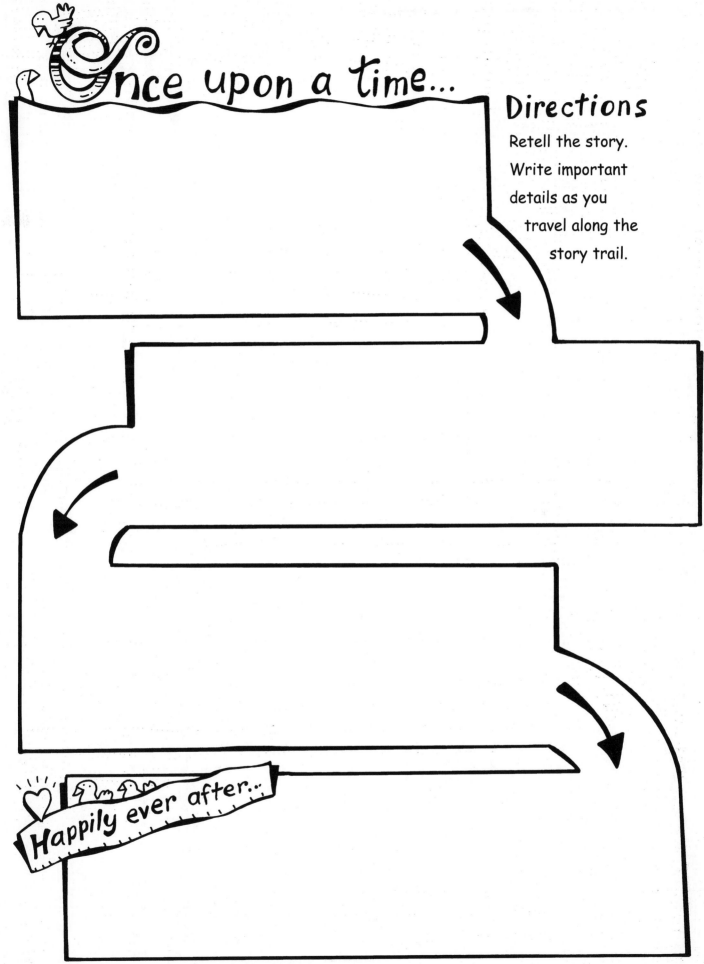

Once upon a time...

Directions

Retell the story. Write important details as you travel along the story trail.

Happily ever after...

DIRECTIONS

Choose 2 fairy tales to compare and contrast. Write each title in a castle. Write about and draw their similarities in the middle tower. Write about and draw their differences in the outer castles.

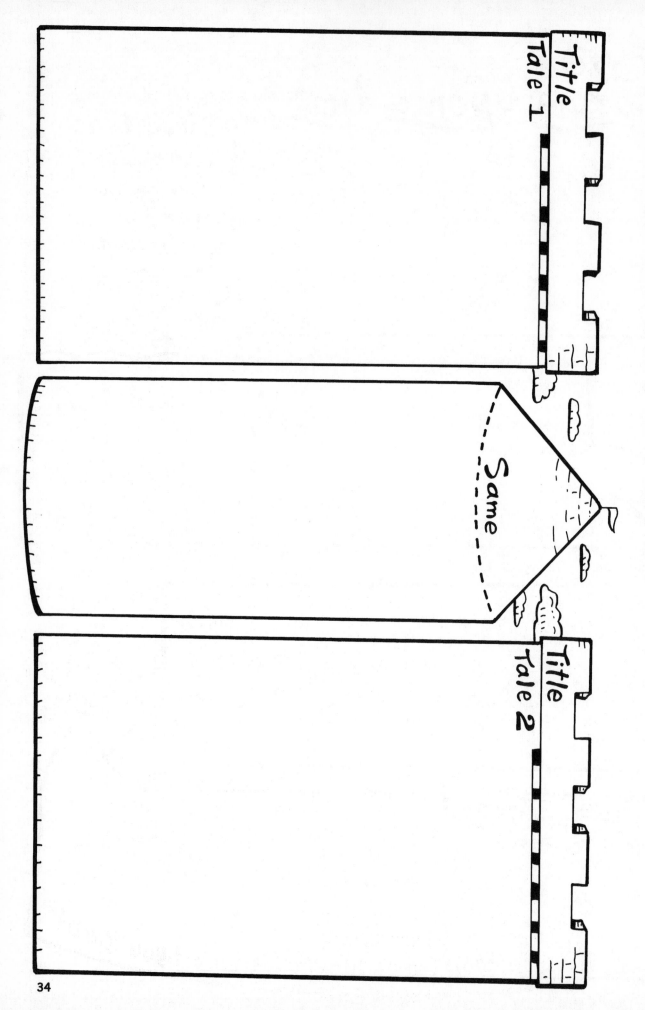

Title

Tale 1

Same

Title

Tale 2

Scholastic Teaching Resources • Grades 2–3 Graphic Organizing Booklet • Fairy Tales, page 5

Personal
★ ★ ★
Response

Use the stars to rate the fairy tale.
Explain why you gave it that rating.

★----------------Ok
★ ★----------Good
★ ★ ★----------Great
★ ★ ★ ★----------Wow!

Rating: Explain:

What did the fairy tale teach? What lesson did you learn?

Helpful Hints for Fables/Tales Booklet:

- Model each activity as many times as necessary to ensure that students fully understand objectives and directions before working independently or in groups.

- Remind students to preview the booklet to be sure they are aware of pre-reading, during-reading, and post-reading activities. For example on page 2, when completing the Character Analysis Chart, students may wish to keep it handy during reading. The chart doesn't require complete sentences. However, discuss the choices, and reasons behind them, to enhance student understanding.

- Encourage reflection and discussion.

Exemplary text: *Mufaro's Beautiful Daughters* by John Steptoe (William Morrow & Company, 1987)

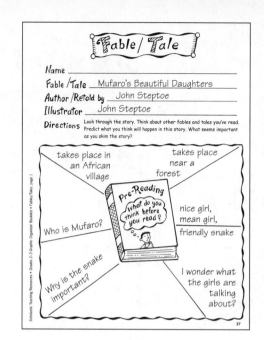

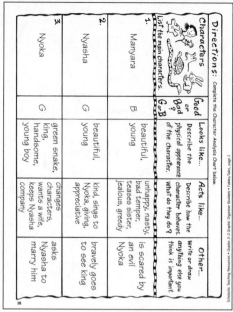

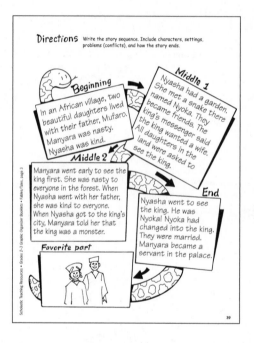

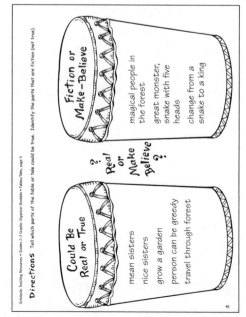

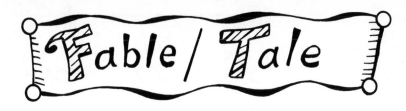

Fable / Tale

Name _____

Fable / Tale _____

Author / Retold by _____

Illustrator _____

Directions Look through the story. Think about other fables and tales you've read. Predict what you think will happen in this story. What seems important as you skim the story?

Directions: Complete the Character Analysis Chart below.

Characters	Good or Bad? G or B	Looks like... Describe the physical appearance of the character.	Acts like... Describe how the character behaves. What do they do?	Other... Write or draw anything else you think is important.
List the main characters.				
1.				
2.				
3.				

Directions
Write the story sequence. Include characters, settings, problems (conflicts), and how the story ends.

Beginning

Middle 1

Middle 2

End

Favorite part

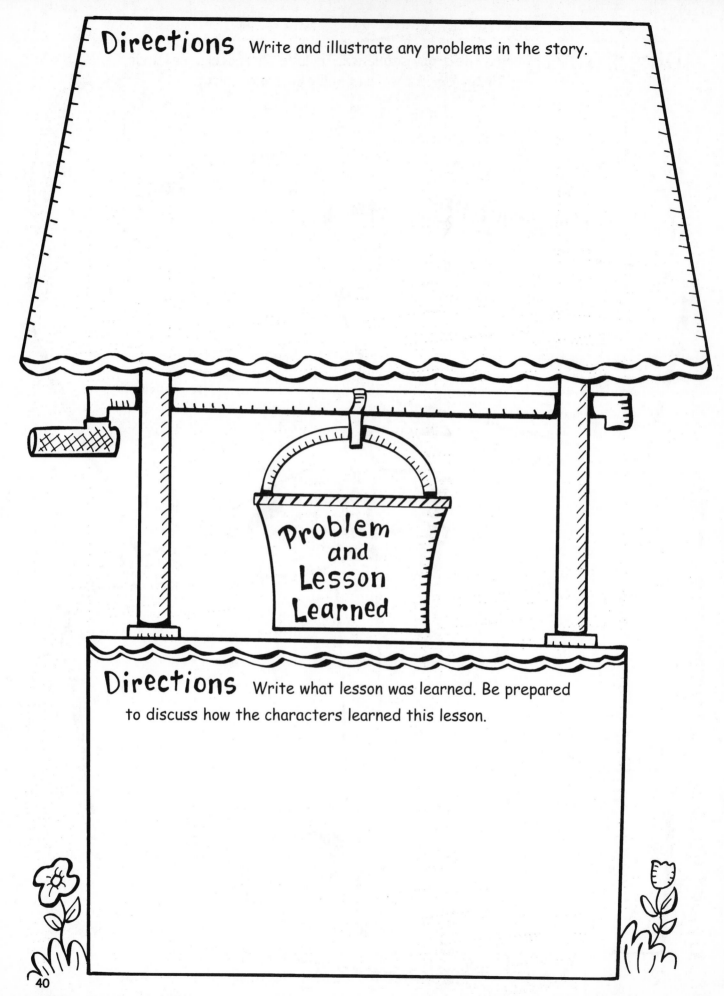

Directions Write and illustrate any problems in the story.

Problem
and
Lesson
Learned

Directions Write what lesson was learned. Be prepared to discuss how the characters learned this lesson.

Scholastic Teaching Resources • Grades 2–3 Graphic Organizer Booklets • Fables/Tales, page 4

Directions Tell which parts of the fable or tale could be true. Identify the parts that are fiction (not true).

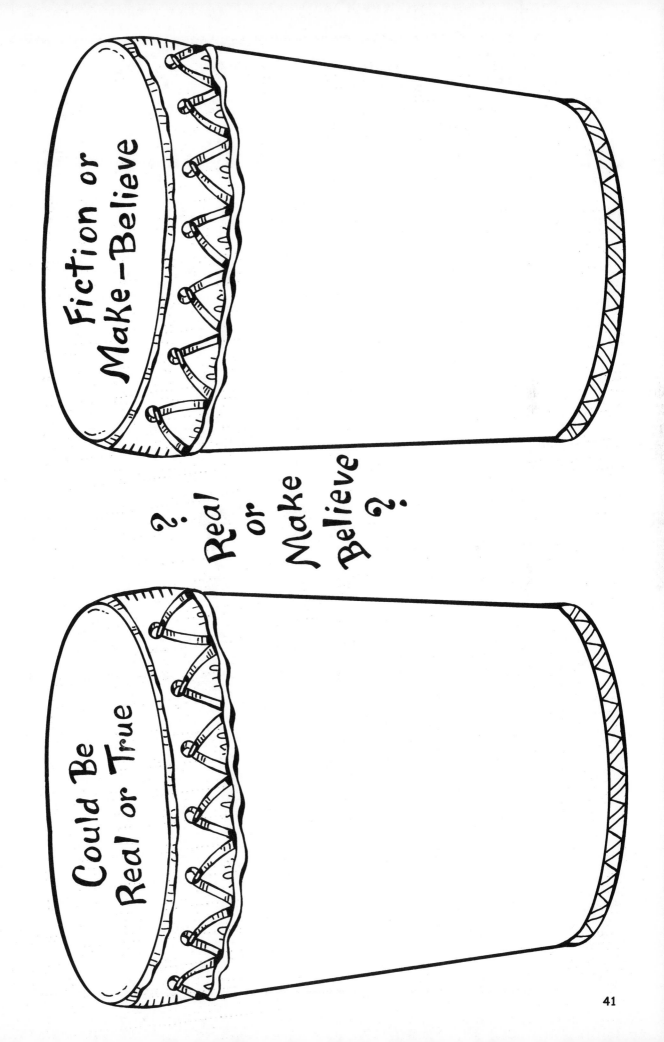

Fiction or Make-Believe

? Real or Make Believe ?

Could Be Real or True

Personal Notes of Interest

Directions: Write your personal response to the story.

How does the lesson relate to your life? Illustrate a story highlight.

Scholastic Teaching Resources • Grades 2–3 Graphic Organizer Booklets • Fables/Tales, page 6

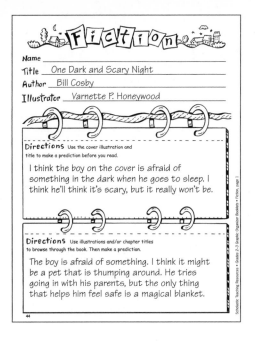

Fiction

Name _____

Title One Dark and Scary Night

Author Bill Cosby

Illustrator Varnette P. Honeywood

Directions Use the cover illustration and title to make a prediction before you read.

I think the boy on the cover is afraid of something in the dark when he goes to sleep. I think he'll think it's scary, but it really won't be.

Directions Use illustrations and/or chapter titles to browse through the book. Then make a prediction.

The boy is afraid of something. I think it might be a pet that is thumping around. He tries going in with his parents, but the only thing that helps him feel safe is a magical blanket.

44

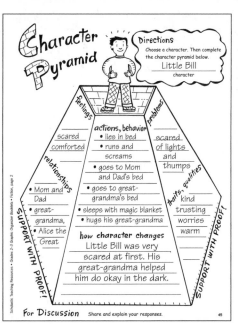

Character Pyramid

Directions Choose a character. Then complete the character pyramid below.

Little Bill
character

feelings
scared
comforted

relationships
• Mom and Dad
• great-grandma,
• Alice the Great

actions, behavior
• lies in bed
• runs and screams
• goes to Mom and Dad's bed
• goes to great-grandma's bed
• sleeps with magic blanket
• hugs his great-grandma

problems
scared of lights and thumps

traits, qualities
kind
trusting
worries
warm

how character changes
Little Bill was very scared at first. His great-grandma helped him do okay in the dark.

SUPPORT WITH PROOF!

For Discussion Share and explain your responses.

45

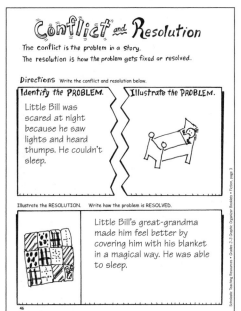

Conflict and Resolution

The conflict is the problem in a story.
The resolution is how the problem gets fixed or resolved.

Directions Write the conflict and resolution below.

Identify the PROBLEM.

Little Bill was scared at night because he saw lights and heard thumps. He couldn't sleep.

Illustrate the PROBLEM.

Illustrate the RESOLUTION.   **Write how the problem is RESOLVED.**

Little Bill's great-grandma made him feel better by covering him with his blanket in a magical way. He was able to sleep.

46

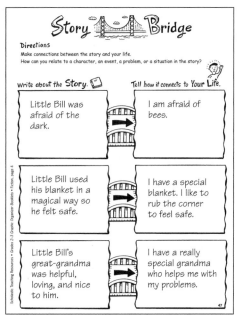

Story Bridge

Directions
Make connections between the story and your life.
How can you relate to a character, an event, a problem, or a situation in the story?

Write about the Story.   **Tell how it connects to Your Life.**

Little Bill was afraid of the dark.

I am afraid of bees.

Little Bill used his blanket in a magical way so he felt safe.

I have a special blanket. I like to rub the corner to feel safe.

Little Bill's great-grandma was helpful, loving, and nice to him.

I have a really special grandma who helps me with my problems.

47

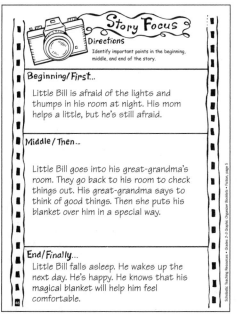

Story Focus

Directions Identify important points in the beginning, middle, and end of the story.

Beginning/First...

Little Bill is afraid of the lights and thumps in his room at night. His mom helps a little, but he's still afraid.

Middle/Then...

Little Bill goes into his great-grandma's room. They go back to his room to check things out. His great-grandma says to think of good things. Then she puts his blanket over him in a special way.

End/Finally...

Little Bill falls asleep. He wakes up the next day. He's happy. He knows that his magical blanket will help him feel comfortable.

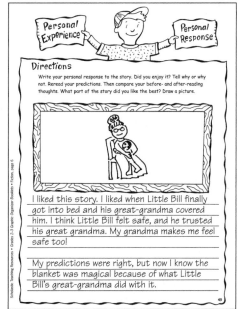

Personal Experience   **Personal Response**

Directions
Write your personal response to the story. Did you enjoy it? Tell why or why not. Reread your predictions. Then compare your before- and after-reading thoughts. What part of the story did you like the best? Draw a picture.

I liked this story. I liked when Little Bill finally got into bed and his great-grandma covered him. I think Little Bill felt safe, and he trusted his great grandma. My grandma makes me feel safe too!

My predictions were right, but now I know the blanket was magical because of what Little Bill's great-grandma did with it.

49

Helpful Hints for the Fiction Booklet:

- Model each activity to make sure that students fully understand objectives and directions before working independently or in groups.

- Remind students to preview the booklet so they are aware of pre-reading, during-reading, and post-reading activities.

- Making predictions after browsing through the story helps students gather important pre-reading information, which activates prior knowledge.

- On page 4, encourage students to think about the story so they can make personal connections. Sometimes students don't see connections right away, but through discussion and example they begin to see how to relate to the text more meaningfully.

- On page 5, review key sequence words and transitional words to aid in retelling.

- On page 6, remind students to refer back to the predictions they made on page 1.

Exemplary text: *One Dark and Scary Night* (A Little Bill Book for Beginning Readers) by Bill Cosby (Scholastic, 1999)

Fiction

Name _____

Title _____

Author _____

Illustrator _____

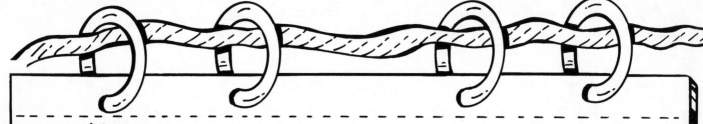

Directions Use the cover illustration and title to make a prediction before you read.

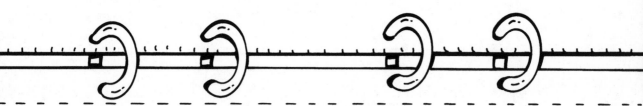

Directions Use illustrations and/or chapter titles to browse through the book. Then make a prediction.

Scholastic Teaching Resources • Grades 2–3 Graphic Organizer Booklets • Fiction, page 1

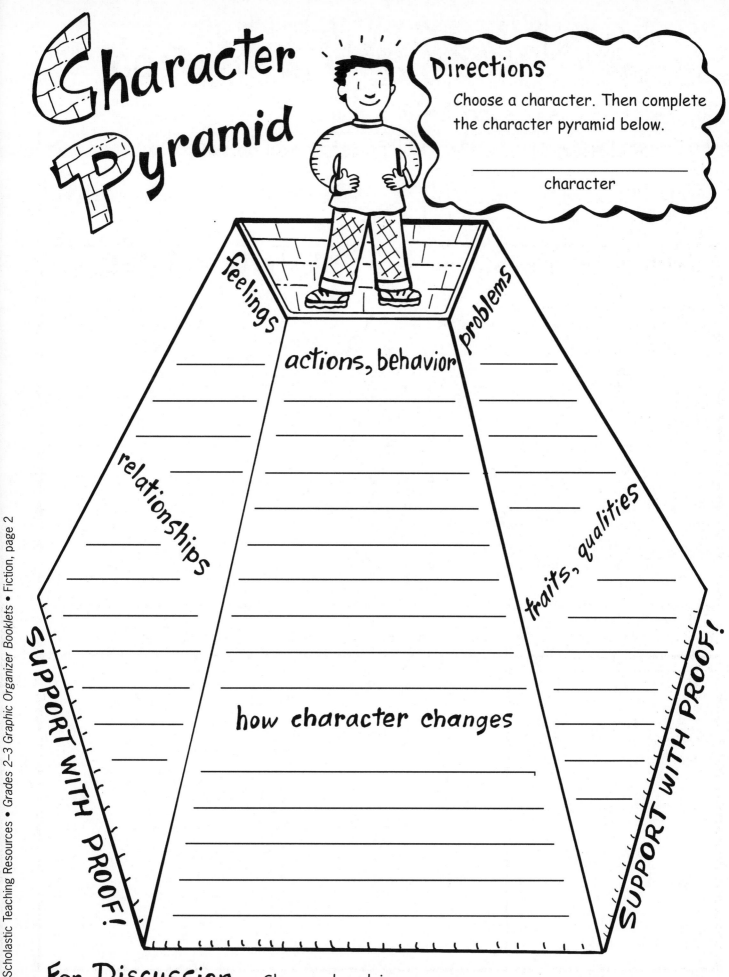

Character Pyramid

Directions

Choose a character. Then complete the character pyramid below.

_____
character

feelings

actions, behavior

problems

relationships

traits, qualities

how character changes

SUPPORT WITH PROOF!

SUPPORT WITH PROOF!

For Discussion
Share and explain your responses.

Conflict and Resolution

The conflict is the problem in a story.

The resolution is how the problem gets fixed or resolved.

Directions Write the conflict and resolution below.

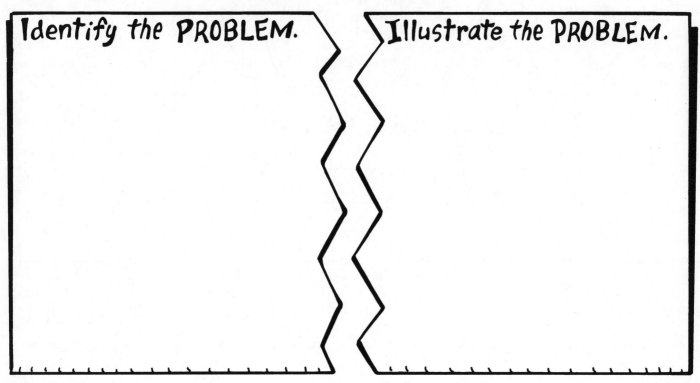

Identify the PROBLEM.   Illustrate the PROBLEM.

Illustrate the RESOLUTION.   Write how the problem is RESOLVED.

Scholastic Teaching Resources • Grades 2–3 Graphic Organizer Booklets • Fiction, page 3

Story  Bridge

Directions

Make connections between the story and your life.

How can you relate to a character, an event, a problem, or a situation in the story?

Write about the **Story.**   Tell how it connects to Your Life.

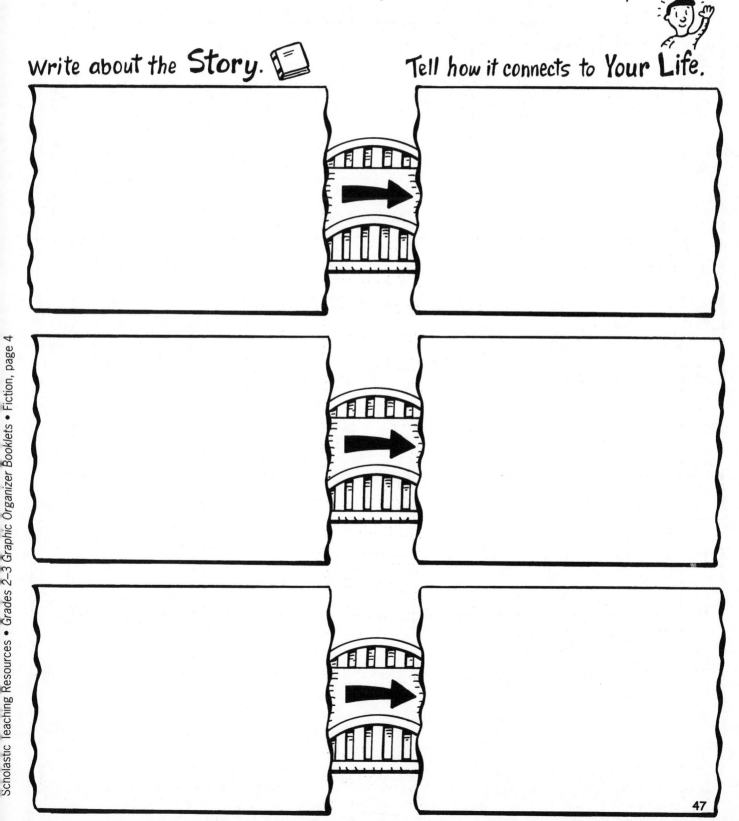

Story Focus

Directions

Identify important points in the beginning, middle, and end of the story.

Beginning/First...

Middle/Then...

End/Finally...

Scholastic Teaching Resources • Grades 2–3 Graphic Organizer Booklets • Fiction, page 5

Personal Experience

Personal Response

Directions

Write your personal response to the story. Did you enjoy it? Tell why or why not. Reread your predictions. Then compare your before- and after-reading thoughts. What part of the story did you like the best? Draw a picture.

Helpful Hints for the Fiction Booklet:

- Model each activity as often as necessary to ensure that students fully understand objectives and directions before working independently or in groups.

- Remind students to preview the booklet to be sure they are aware of pre-reading, during-reading, and post-reading activities. For example, be sure students go back to check their predictions and "I wonder…" statements on page 1.

- On page 2, have students share questions and then respond to the group discussion. The importance of this part of the activity is to engage in reflective thinking. (This may require extra modeling!)

Exemplary text: *Ruby the Copycat* by Peggy Rathmann (Scholastic, 1991)

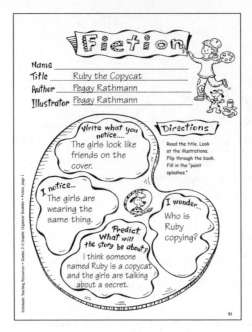

Fiction

Name _____
Title _____ Ruby the Copycat
Author _____ Peggy Rathmann
Illustrator _____ Peggy Rathmann

Directions
Read the title. Look at the illustrations. Flip through the book. Fill in the "paint splashes."

Write what you notice....
The girls look like friends on the cover.

I notice...
The girls are wearing the same thing.

I wonder...
Who is Ruby copying?

Predict
What will the story be about?
I think someone named Ruby is a copycat and the girls are talking about a secret.

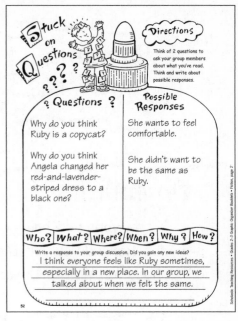

Stuck on Questions ???

Directions
Think of 2 questions to ask your group members about what you've read. Think and write about possible responses.

? Questions ?

Why do you think Ruby is a copycat?

Why do you think Angela changed her red-and-lavender-striped dress to a black one?

Possible Responses

She wants to feel comfortable.

She didn't want to be the same as Ruby.

| Who? | What? | Where? | When? | Why? | How? |

Write a response to your group discussion. Did you gain any new ideas?
I think everyone feels like Ruby sometimes, especially in a new place. In our group, we talked about when we felt the same.

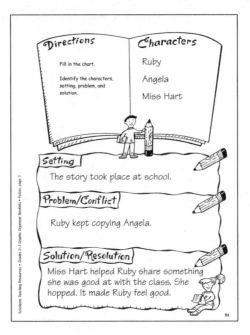

Directions
Fill in the chart.
Identify the characters, setting, problem, and solution.

Characters
Ruby
Angela
Miss Hart

Setting
The story took place at school.

Problem/Conflict
Ruby kept copying Angela.

Solution/Resolution
Miss Hart helped Ruby share something she was good at with the class. She hopped. It made Ruby feel good.

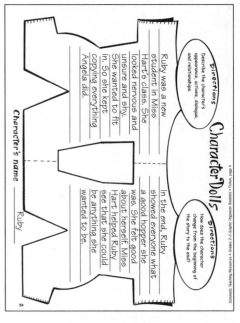

Character Dolls

Directions
Describe the character's appearance, actions, dialogue, and relationships.

Ruby was a new student in Miss Hart's class. She looked nervous and unsure and shy. She wanted to fit in. So she kept copying everything Angela did.

Directions
How does the character change from the beginning of the story to the end?

In the end, Ruby showed everyone what a good hopper she was. She felt good about herself. Miss Hart helped Ruby see that she could be anything she wanted to be.

Character's name _____ Ruby

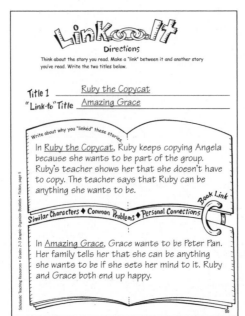

Link-It

Directions
Think about the story you read. Make a "link" between it and another story you've read. Write the two titles below.

Title 1 _____ Ruby the Copycat
"Link-to" Title _____ Amazing Grace

Write about why you "linked" these stories.
In Ruby the Copycat, Ruby keeps copying Angela because she wants to be part of the group. Ruby's teacher shows her that she doesn't have to copy. The teacher says that Ruby can be anything she wants to be.

Similar Characters ◆ Common Problems ◆ Personal Connections

In Amazing Grace, Grace wants to be Peter Pan. Her family tells her that she can be anything she wants to be if she sets her mind to it. Ruby and Grace both end up happy.

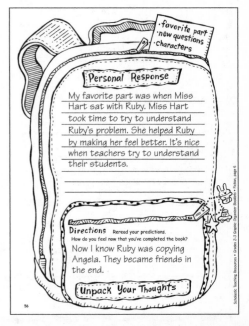

- favorite part
- new questions
- characters

Personal Response
My favorite part was when Miss Hart sat with Ruby. Miss Hart took time to try to understand Ruby's problem. She helped Ruby by making her feel better. It's nice when teachers try to understand their students.

Directions Reread your predictions. How do you feel now that you've completed the book?
Now I know Ruby was copying Angela. They became friends in the end.

Unpack Your Thoughts

Fiction

Name _____

Title _____

Author _____

Illustrator _____

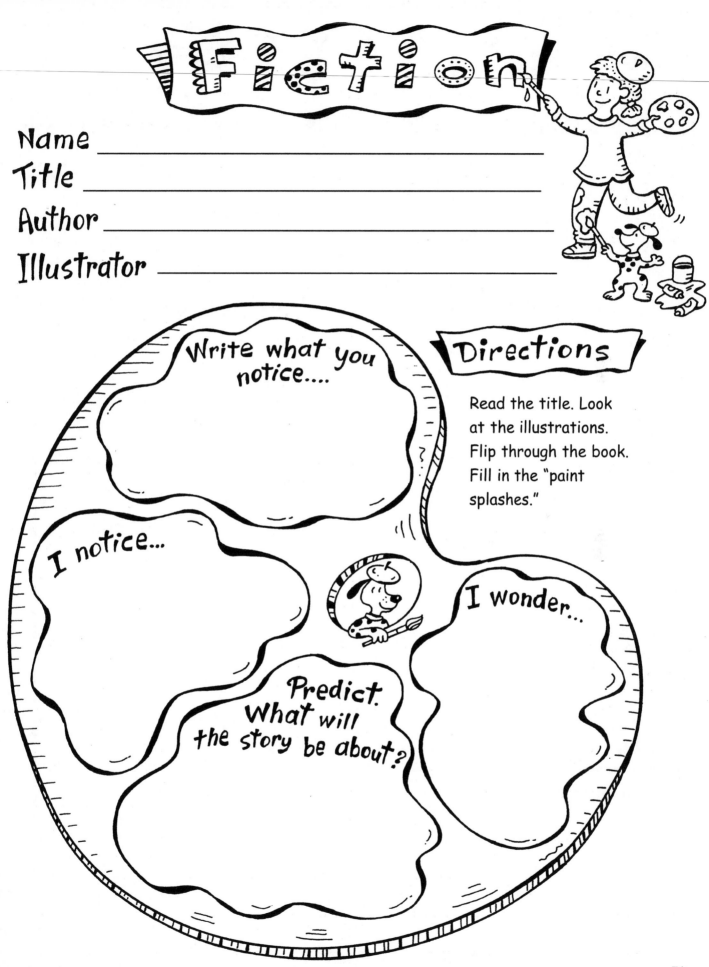

Write what you notice....

I notice...

I wonder...

Predict. What will the story be about?

Directions

Read the title. Look at the illustrations. Flip through the book. Fill in the "paint splashes."

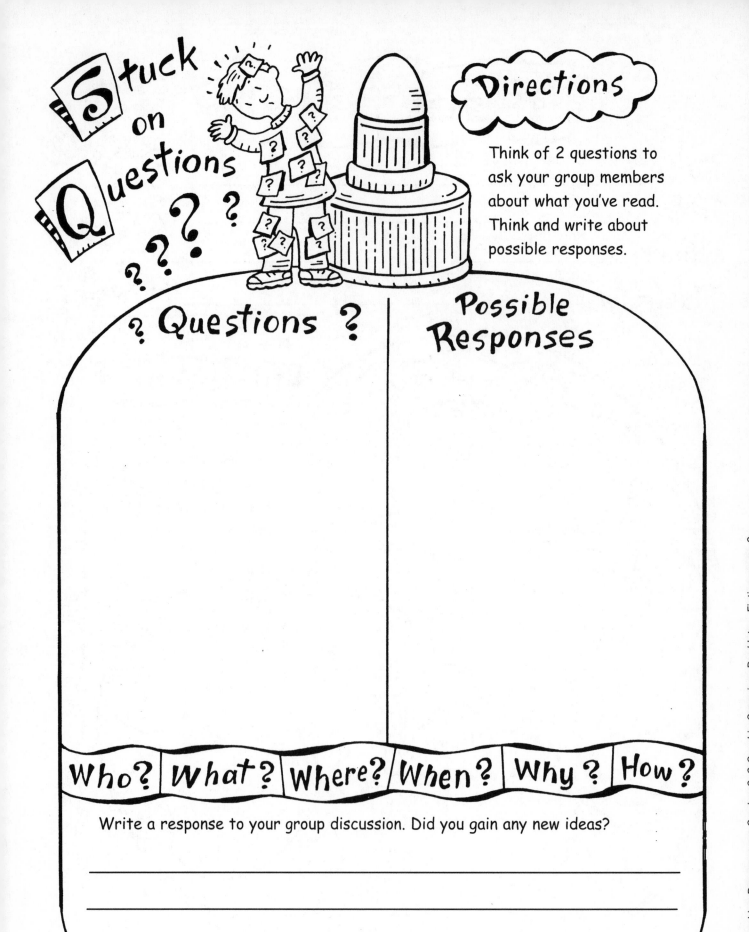

Stuck on Questions

Directions

Think of 2 questions to ask your group members about what you've read. Think and write about possible responses.

? Questions ?	Possible Responses

Who? What? Where? When? Why? How?

Write a response to your group discussion. Did you gain any new ideas?

_____

_____

_____

_____

Scholastic Teaching Resources • Grades 2–3 Graphic Organizer Booklets • Fiction, page 2

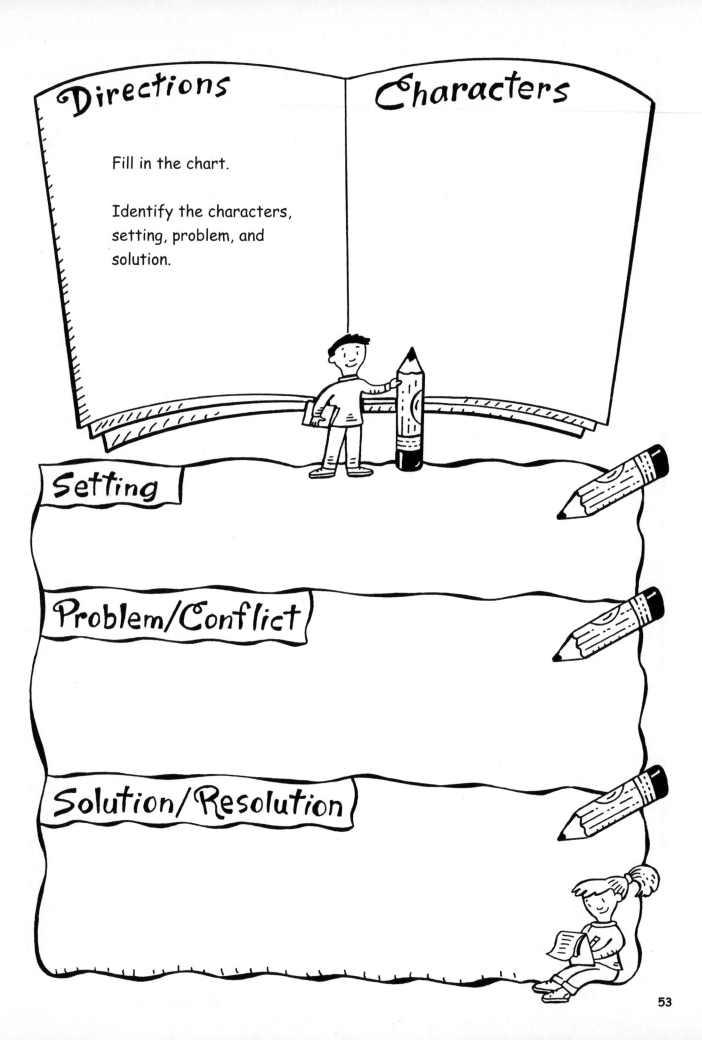

Directions

Characters

Fill in the chart.

Identify the characters, setting, problem, and solution.

Setting

Problem/Conflict

Solution/Resolution

Scholastic Teaching Resources • Grades 2–3 Graphic Organizer Booklets • Fiction, page 3

CharacterDolls

Character's name ___

Directions

Describe the character's appearance, actions, dialogue, and relationships.

Directions

How does the character change from the beginning of the story to the end?

Directions

Think about the story you read. Make a "link" between it and another story you've read. Write the two titles below.

Title 1 _____

"Link-to" Title _____

Write about why you "linked" these stories.

Similar Characters ◆ Common Problems ◆ Personal Connections

Book Link

Scholastic Teaching Resources • Grades 2–3 Graphic Organizer Booklets • Fiction, page 5

·favorite part
·new questions
·characters

Personal Response

Directions   Reread your predictions.
How do you feel now that you've completed the book?

Unpack Your Thoughts

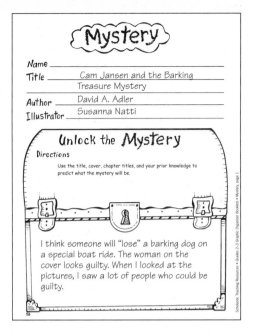

Mystery

Name _____
Title _____ Cam Jansen and the Barking
_____ Treasure Mystery
Author _____ David A. Adler
Illustrator _____ Susanna Natti

Unlock the Mystery

Directions

Use the title, cover, chapter titles, and your prior knowledge to predict what the mystery will be.

I think someone will "lose" a barking dog on a special boat ride. The woman on the cover looks guilty. When I looked at the pictures, I saw a lot of people who could be guilty.

58

Directions

Get to know the detective. Complete the "sleuth web" by writing information about the detective.

Friends and Relationships
Eric Shelton (friend)
Lila (woman with dog)
Little Treasure (lost dog)

Sleuth
Cam Jansen

Appearance, Physical description
young girl
freckles
hair to shoulders

Problems the detective faces
She has to find the dog before the boat ride ends.

Additional Notes about the Detective
She has a photographic memory "click."
Her real name is Jennifer.
Cam comes from "camera" because of her memory.

59

Directions

In the magnifying glass, answer this question: What is the mystery that has to be solved?

The woman in the red dress had a pet dog named Little Treasure. The dog had a fancy collar. The woman snuck Little Treasure on the boat. Then the dog disappeared.

The mystery takes place on a sightseeing boat that goes around the city.

Directions

In the handle, describe the setting of the mystery. Think about time, place, and changes in setting.

60

Who Done It?

Directions

Use the footprints to keep track of the characters. Who are the suspects?

In each heel, write the name of a character. In the top part of the footprint, write important information about that character.

- near woman in red dress
- carrying a cloth bag

thin man with bushy beard
character 1

- near woman in red dress
- carrying a shopping bag
- standing at back of boat, not sightseeing like everyone else

short, bald man
character 2

- near woman in red dress
- wrong woman getting drink

woman with long blond hair, earrings
character 3

- near woman in red dress
- puffy jacket to hide dog
- sitting next to a woman, holding hands

man with orange baseball cap
character 4

61

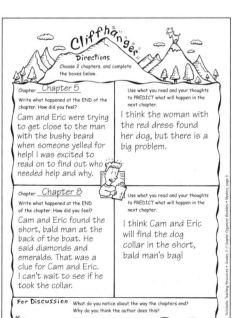

Cliffhanger

Directions

Choose 2 chapters, and complete the boxes below.

Chapter __Chapter 5__

Write what happened at the END of the chapter. How did you feel?

Cam and Eric were trying to get close to the man with the bushy beard when someone yelled for help! I was excited to read on to find out who needed help and why.

Use what you read and your thoughts to PREDICT what will happen in the next chapter.

I think the woman with the red dress found her dog, but there is a big problem.

Chapter __Chapter 8__

Write what happened at the END of the chapter. How did you feel?

Cam and Eric found the short, bald man at the back of the boat. He said diamonds and emeralds. That was a clue for Cam and Eric. I can't wait to see if he took the collar.

Use what you read and your thoughts to PREDICT what will happen in the next chapter.

I think Cam and Eric will find the dog collar in the short, bald man's bag!

For Discussion What do you notice about the way the chapters end? Why do you think the author does this?

62

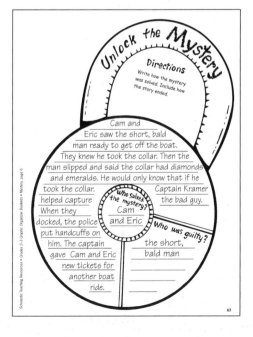

Unlock the Mystery

Directions

Write how the mystery was solved. Include how the story ended.

Cam and Eric saw the short, bald man ready to get off the boat. They knew he took the collar. Then the man slipped and said the collar had diamonds and emeralds. He would only know that if he took the collar. Cam and Eric helped capture When they docked, the police put handcuffs on him. The captain gave Cam and Eric new tickets for another boat ride.

Who solved the mystery?
Cam and Eric

Captain Kramer the bad guy.

Who was guilty?
the short, bald man
_____
_____

63

Helpful Hints for the Mystery Booklet:

- Model each activity as many times as necessary to ensure that students fully understand objectives and directions before working independently or in groups.

- Remind students to preview the booklet to be sure they are aware of pre-reading, during-reading, and post-reading activities.

- This booklet should be handy during reading so students can record subtle clues and hints sprinkled throughout the mystery. Recording this information will help them organize their thoughts. Often mysteries can become confusing because there are multiple suspects and misleading clues.

- On page 5, students must choose two chapters ahead of time. The goal is to show how the author leaves the reader hanging and wanting to read more. Help students recognize how the author does this.

Exemplary text: *Cam Jansen and the Barking Treasure Mystery* by David A. Adler (Viking Children's Books, 1999)

Mystery

Name _____

Title _____

_____

Author _____

Illustrator _____

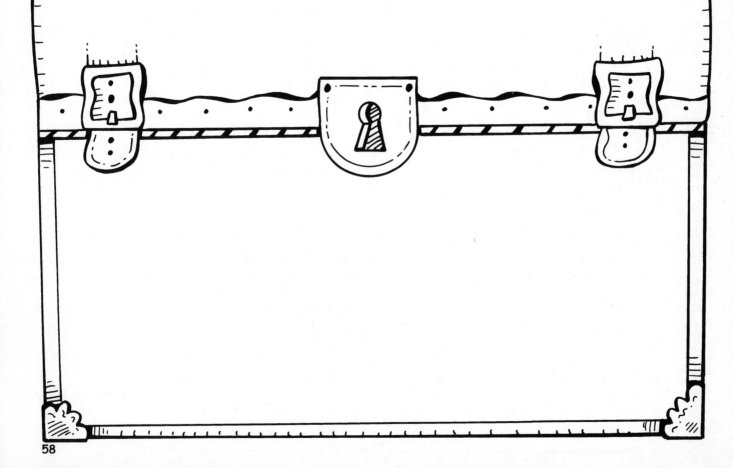

Unlock the Mystery

Directions

Use the title, cover, chapter titles, and your prior knowledge to predict what the mystery will be.

58

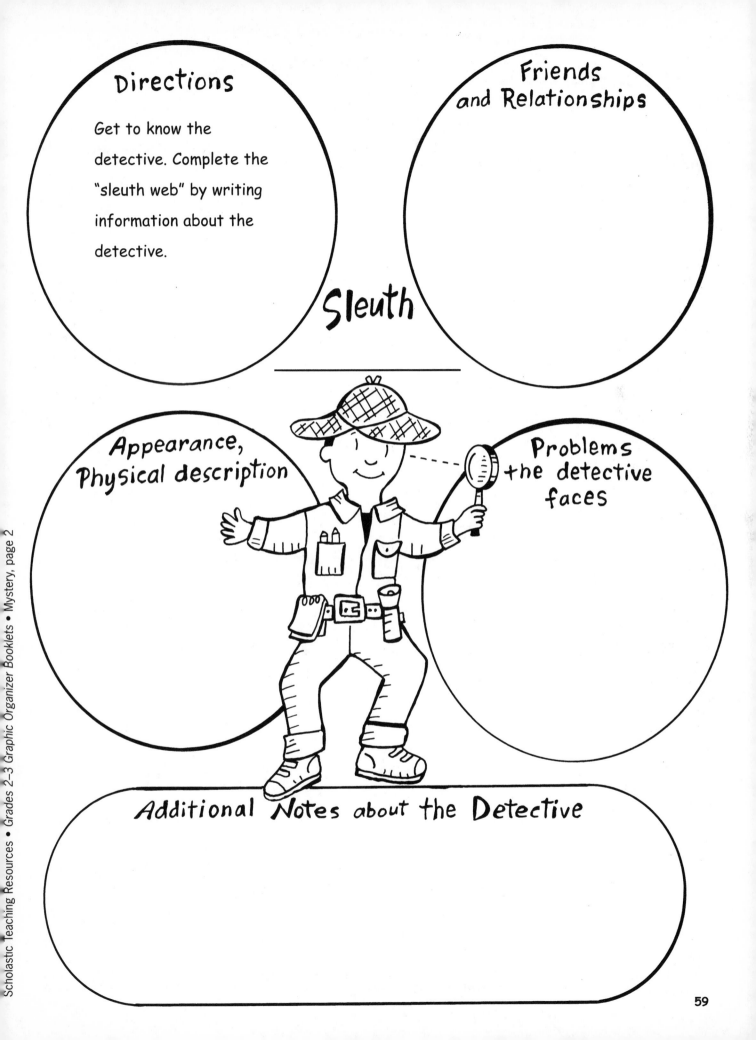

Directions

Get to know the detective. Complete the "sleuth web" by writing information about the detective.

Friends and Relationships

Sleuth

_____

Appearance, Physical description

Problems the detective faces

Additional Notes about the Detective

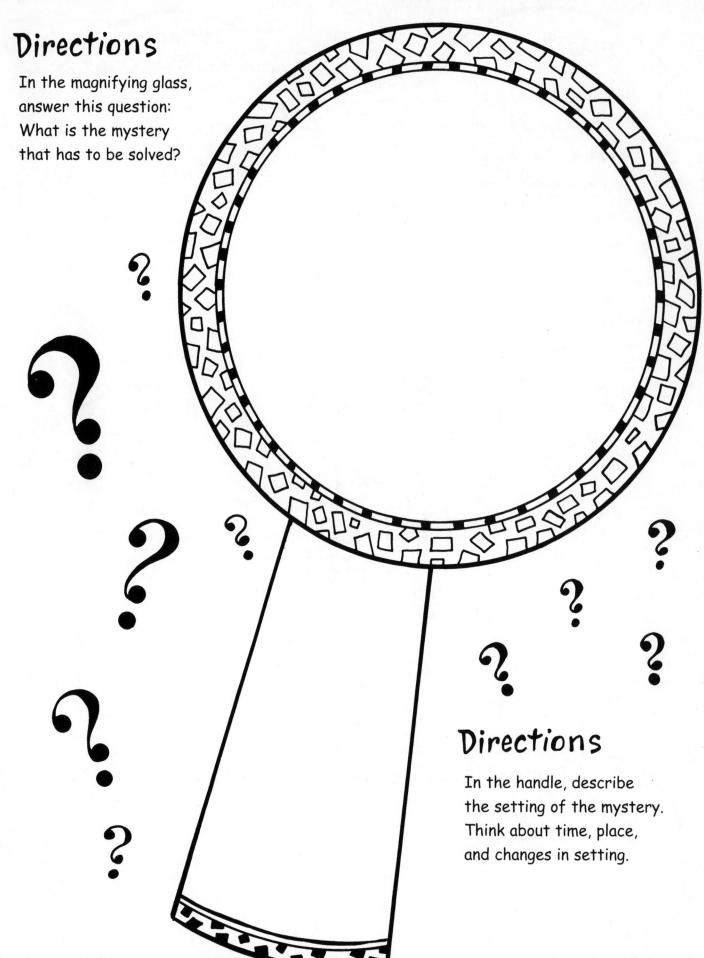

Directions

In the magnifying glass, answer this question: What is the mystery that has to be solved?

Directions

In the handle, describe the setting of the mystery. Think about time, place, and changes in setting.

Who Done It?

Directions

Use the footprints to keep track of the characters. Who are the suspects?

In each heel, write the name of a character. In the top part of the footprint, write important information about that character.

character 1

character 2

character 3

character 4

Scholastic Teaching Resources • Grades 2–3 Graphic Organizer Booklets • Mystery, page 4

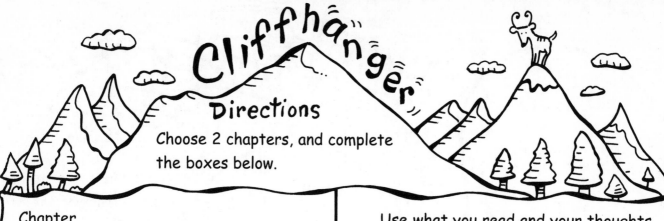

Directions

Choose 2 chapters, and complete the boxes below.

Chapter _____

Write what happened at the END of the chapter. How did you feel?

Use what you read and your thoughts to PREDICT what will happen in the next chapter.

Chapter _____

Write what happened at the END of the chapter. How did you feel?

Use what you read and your thoughts to PREDICT what will happen in the next chapter.

For Discussion

What do you notice about the way the chapters end?
Why do you think the author does this?

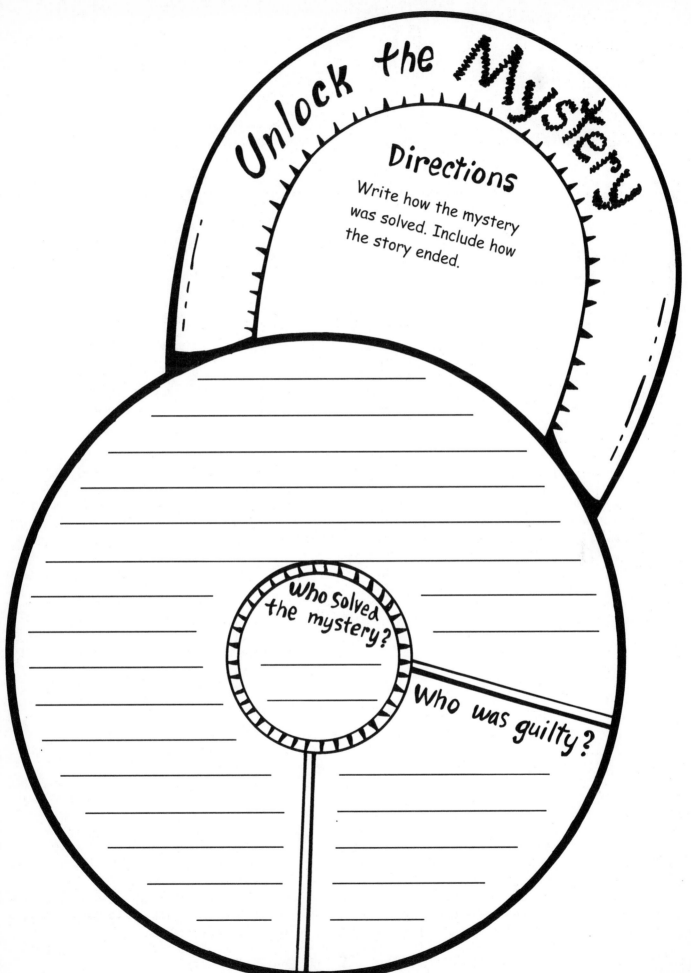

Unlock the Mystery

Directions

Write how the mystery was solved. Include how the story ended.

Who Solved the mystery?

Who was guilty?

Notes